To the reader:

The main facts of the following story are true. Because the events of the story took place so long ago, nobody knows all the details. Therefore, I have taken certain liberties with a few of the facts. Many of the dialogues are of my own invention.

AJW

Chapter One

All was quiet in the little village. Snow was falling, and the wind beat down on the poor cabins and tents. The night was dark; only a dim light shone in the window of one of the cabins.

The cabin was one large room. The people who lived there had hung blankets to make two rooms out of it. In the smaller of the rooms, two men sat and talked. They said little – there were long pauses between their talking. The men looked very old and tired. They had seen a lot of suffering in their times, and it showed in their dark faces. They were cold, as the wind blew through the cabin. They covered themselves with blankets and drank tea to keep warm.

"What more do the white men want, Standing Bear?" asked the older of the two men. "They have already killed all our buffalo and taken our land. Now they are taking our children."

"Not all white men are bad, Buffalo Chip. And they are not killing us now. It is sickness that takes our people."

"White men's sickness takes our people," said Buffalo Chip. "Before the white men came, we were happy and we were healthy. Now we know only sickness and death."

After a minute of silence, Standing Bear answered. "The white men have taught us many things, Buffalo Chip. They have taught us about their God, who is a better God than ours. And that God tells us to forgive."

"I have forgiven a lot of things, Standing Bear. But where will it end?"

Standing Bear lit his pipe and passed it to his friend. Buffalo Chip knew that Standing Bear did not want to talk any more, so he said nothing and smoked. There was a comfortable silence between the two men. They had known each other for a long time, and they had gone through many things together. They did not need words to know what the other was feeling.

After a few moments, a woman came into the room. Like the men, she looked old and weak, and she wore blankets to keep warm. Her eyes were sad as she spoke to her husband.

"Standing Bear, it is time."

Standing Bear puffed on his pipe for a moment, then slowly got up. His bones made crunching sounds as he stood up, and his 50 years weighed on him heavily. He tried to look strong, but he, too, looked sad and frightened.

"He has asked for you, Standing Bear," said the woman. And again, "It is time."

The old man suddenly looked a hundred years old. But he nodded, then walked into the next room, where a small fire burned on the dirt floor. It was a little warmer there, and Standing Bear dropped the blankets he had been holding around him to keep warm.

He stood as tall as he could and tried to look strong and brave. Then he walked toward the bed, where a young man was lying under five buffalo skins. The young man looked like he had once been very big and strong, but now his bones looked like they wanted to come out of his skin.

"Son," said the chief, "you have asked for me."

"Yes, father. It is time."

"You have been a good son, and I pray to God that He will know that."

"What God do you pray to, father? Ours or theirs?"

"There is only one God, son. He made the people, and He made the white men. He made some men good and some bad."

"Father, I do not want to argue with you. I only wanted to say goodbye."

With tears in his eyes, Standing Bear took his son's cold hand. "You will get better, son. I know it."

"No, father, this is the end. – Please, listen to me, father. When I am gone, I want you to take my bones back to the place where I was born. I want to be buried in the land of my fathers."

"I understand, son. It will be done."

But the boy did not hear his father's last words. He had died, just as over 150 of his tribe had done in the year since they had been forced to move to Indian Territory. It had been the same for all of them. They became sick and weak, could not eat any more. After a time, they could not even keep down the drinks the medicine man gave them. They suffered from fever, then chills. And then their suffering was over.

The old chief held his dead son in his arms for several minutes, then laid him out to look like he was sleeping. He sat on the side of his son's bed and thought about things. He thought about the three laws of his people for their chiefs. Be good to the old. Be good to the orphans. Be good to the needy. But there were so many orphans now, so many needy people. How could he possibly be good to all of them? How could he go on as their chief?

He thought about *xúbe,* the power men get as they get older. *Xúbe* was a special power in all older men. It was there to help them when their physical powers began to fail. It was there to help them through situations like this. No, he was not going to give up, he decided. Life would go on better than before.

The chief tried to look especially brave before returning to his wife, but she saw in his face that their son was dead. But she was too weak from the many months of looking after the sick to cry. Standing Bear took his wife in his arms and cried for both of them.

After he had stopped crying, his wife said bitterly, "We have already lost a daughter here, and now our son. Are we going to wait for our last child to die, too?"

"No," answered Standing Bear loudly. "We will wait no longer. Buffalo Chip, I will have a meeting of my lodge. We will meet in the main cabin in a few minutes. If you want, bring the people from your lodge, too. I have something important to say."

Standing Bear with his wife, Suzette, and his grandson, Walk in the Wind

Chapter Two

There was much excitement in the village the next day. Standing Bear had announced at the meeting the night before that he and his family were returning to the land of their fathers. Anyone who wanted to go with them could do so.

"The white men will try to stop us, my friends," he had said.

"They have forced us to move here, and they will not want us to go back. They will send soldiers. The soldiers have always treated us fairly, but they will kill us if they are told to do so.

"Everyone here is sick. Every family has lost someone to sickness since we came here. I have lost most of my children. I have only one little girl left. In a few weeks, she, too, will be dead.

"I am returning to the land of our fathers, and I will take anyone with me who wants to go. Yes, the soldiers will come after us. I will not fight them. My warriors are too sick and weak to fight. And the soldiers have always been good to us. I could not kill them. Let them do anything they want to us. It cannot be worse than staying here.

"I will leave as soon as it gets dark again tomorrow. The white men here at the agency will not miss us until the next day. Then they will tell the soldiers to look for us. If God thinks we are doing the right thing, He will protect us, and we will find our way home."

Some of the younger members of the lodge were very angry. "Before the white men made us come here, we asked you to fight. You did not, and our people are dying. Even now, you say you will not fight. You call yourself chief?"

"I do not call myself chief any more," answered Standing Bear. "I am not better than any of you. We are all here, we are all poor, and many of us are dying. My children are dead or dying. No, I am not better than any of you. I am no longer chief.

"And I do not *tell* anyone to go with me. I say only that I am going back to the land of our fathers. If anyone wants to come with me, they can. But they must promise me that they will not fight the soldiers if they come. That is all. The meeting is over."

After Standing Bear left the meeting, the people of his lodge sat in silence. No one moved. Had they heard correctly? Had Standing Bear, who had always done what the white men asked, really said he was going to go against the orders of the white men? And had he really said he was no longer their chief? Who would look after them if they no longer had a chief?

All these questions and more rested heavily on the minds of the Poncas who had come to the meeting that January 1, 1879. Most left the meeting room without saying a word. They went to their cold cabins or tents and talked about what had happened.

In their tent, Du-ba-mo-ni asked her husband, "Do you want me to start packing our things?"

"Don't be a fool, woman," her husband answered. "Standing Bear will have us all killed. Or the soldiers will send us back here to die. No, we are not going."

"You stay here if you want to. If I am going to die, I want to do it in the land where my mother and her mother before her are buried."

"I will not try to stop you, Du-ba-mo-ni. Go if you must. I will stay."

Similar scenes took place in many tents and cabins that night, and the next day there was more of the same. There was much loud discussion in the Ponca camp. The white men at the Indian agency knew something was happening, but no one would tell them what. The Poncas were quiet when the white men were around, although there were no white men there who could understand their language.

When the sun had set and Standing Bear was ready to go, 30 Poncas, 20 from his lodge and ten others, stood outside his cabin. Seven of the group were very ill.

Someone said, "We must leave the sick here; they will slow us down," but Standing Bear disagreed.

"I said I would take everyone who wanted to go, and I will. The sick are Poncas, too, and they wish to go to the land of their fathers."

"But they will be in the way if we have to run from the soldiers," protested Long Runner.

The wise old chief smiled. "If you wish, Long Runner, we will leave you to die if you become sick during the journey." There was no more discussion.

Under the cover of darkness, Standing Bear and his 30 followers said goodbye to the others. Many had tears in their eyes; they did not know whether they would ever see each other again.

Many of those who decided to stay behind had little presents for their friends: food, blankets, money. No one knew how long it would take them to reach the land of their fathers in Nebraska, over 600 miles away. The food they had would last about two weeks. The group also had $20 with them, so they would be able to buy a few things during their journey.

So, with two old, tired horses to pull the wagon that held the trunk with the body of Standing Bear's son, the 31 Poncas started on their journey into the winter night. It was January 2, 1879.

Chapter Three

The first few days of the march, the weather was fairly mild. There was some snow on the ground in places, but most of the time they had to walk through mud. Walking was not easy because the Poncas could not use roads. They stayed away from towns, where white men might see them and tell the soldiers. But everyone was feeling happy – happier than they had felt during the months they had stayed in Indian Territory. Once again, the Poncas were free and out in the wilderness.

Standing Bear and Buffalo Chip walked ahead of the rest. They both felt years younger. "It is almost like old times, Standing Bear," said Buffalo Chip.

"Yes, Buffalo Chip, almost. Remember the great hunts we had? For days at a time, the men left camp to hunt buffaloes. I'll never forget the feasts we had when we came back, the songs of the women and children."

"But now the buffalo are gone ..."

"Yes, but we have learned to become good farmers. The white men showed us these things, and we have done well at them."

"That is true, Standing Bear. But the white men could not stop the Sioux from attacking us and destroying our crops. And then they gave our land away and sent us to Indian Territory like prisoners."

Standing Bear had nothing to say about this because he knew it was true. Although the Poncas and the whites had lived in peace for many years, the whites were now treating them like criminals.

Buffalo Chip stopped walking, and the two men waited for the others. "When we make camp tonight, Standing Bear will tell us a story from the history of the people."

The children in the group were very excited. They remembered how Standing Bear told them stories when they still lived in Nebraska. The old chief was a good storyteller with a beautiful voice. He knew how to make the children laugh. Most of them hadn't been able to laugh for months.

Yes, everything was going to be the way it was again.

That night, when the group made their camp under the huge sky, the stars seemed to be smiling at them. The moon looked down at them and made them feel very much at home, although they did not know this strange land so far from the land of their fathers.

All 31 Poncas sat close around the small fire they had used to warm the fried bread and dried meat that they had with them. They did not want to make a large fire because white men might see it and tell the soldiers they were there. They ate very little because their journey might last a long time. They did not know if they would see any animals to hunt, and they did not know if they would be strong enough to hunt them if they did.

As the fire began to die down, Standing Bear lit his pipe. The children could not sit still because they were waiting for Standing Bear to start his story. He liked to make the children wait. He knew that they would like his story better if they had to wait a little. After a few puffs of his pipe he began his story.

"When He was very young, Wakanda felt very alone. He walked from one end of the earth to the other, but there was no one there for him to talk to or play with. One day, while He was walking, He found a spot that He had never seen before, although He Himself had made it.

"He was very surprised that even He could have made such a beautiful place. The sky seemed bluer there. There were wonderful hills there with lots of animals, and there was lots of water. Two rivers met there. They carried the clearest water Wakanda had ever seen. He decided then and there that these two rivers needed a name. He had not named any other place, but such a beautiful spot needed a name, He thought. After a few minutes, Wakanda made His decision: the larger river would be called Niobrara, the smaller one would be Keya Paha.

" 'But why make such a beautiful place and give names to the rivers if no one else can see this spot or speak these names?' Wakanda asked no one. As soon as He had spoken these words, Wakanda-pezi appeared."

Standing Bear lit his pipe again and looked at the frightened faces of the children. The name Wakanda-pezi always put fear in their faces, like the whistling of the ghosts at night. He smiled a small smile before he continued.

" 'Who are you?' Wakanda asked. He had been walking the earth for a long time, and He had never seen this person.

" 'I am Wakanda-pezi. I came here to see this land and to speak the names of the two rivers.'

" 'But where did you come from? I have never seen you before.'

" 'I came from you, just like this land and everything in it. You wished for someone else to see this land and speak the names of the rivers. Here I am.'

"Wakanda thought about this for a moment, then said, 'If I made you, you must be a good spirit. We will live in this land together. We will name the animals, we can fish and hunt together. We will be friends.'

" 'No, Wakanda. Now that I have seen this land, I want to keep it myself. You must leave.'

"But Wakanda did not want to leave. And, although He tried to make peace with this evil spirit, He could not. He had to find a way to make Wakanda-pezi leave. Then He had an idea.

"Wakanda walked to the spot where the Niobrara and the Keya Paha Rivers met. Wakanda-pezi watched Wakanda as He reached into the Niobrara with one hand, and into the Keya Paha with the other. Wakanda then took the water from both rivers and used it to make mud. He formed the mud until it looked just like Him. Then He breathed on the mud, and it came to life.

"Wakanda-pezi did not understand what was happening. But then he saw how the mud-person and Wakanda started making more mud-people, who made more mud-people, who made more. When there were a hundred mud-people, Wakanda announced, 'I have made the people, the Poncas, and they will share this land with me. Wakanda-pezi, you must go. The Poncas and I will fight, if we have to, to keep you away from here.'

"Wakanda-pezi knew that he had no choice. He could not possibly fight so many people. So he left the land around the Niobrara and Keya Paha. He went to other parts of Wakanda's world, but he still remembers where the most beautiful spot is. He still wants to go back there, to the Niobrara and the Keya Paha. The people must not let him do that."

Standing Bear lit his pipe again. The children knew that Standing Bear would not tell any more stories that night, so they thanked him and went off with their families to sleep. Only Standing Bear and Buffalo Chip stayed by the fire. They sat for a long time, passed the pipe, but did not say anything. After a few moments, Buffalo Chip looked into his friend's eyes and nodded before he, too, left the fire, lay down and covered himself in blankets to sleep.

CHAPTER FOUR

Two weeks into the journey, the weather got worse, and the Poncas ran out of food. They had tried to eat as little as possible, but that had only made them weaker. Now they had to do something fast because the children were crying, and the sick Poncas, who had felt better in the early days of the trip, were becoming sick again.

For two weeks they had tried to stay away from towns and farmhouses out of fear of the white men. Now they had no choice. They would have to go to a white man's house and try to buy some food.

At about noon on the sixteenth day of their journey, they saw a small farmhouse in the middle of a big field. The house looked poor, but to the Poncas it seemed like heaven. Together they walked toward it. A little white girl was carrying a bucket of milk from the barn to the farmhouse when she saw the 31 Indians who were walking toward the house.

Frightened, the girl dropped the bucket, screamed and ran into the house. A few moments later her father stood in the doorway with a shotgun in his hand.

"What do you want?" shouted the man. He pointed his gun straight at Standing Bear.

But no one in the group could speak English. If only my son was here, Standing Bear thought. He spoke the language of the white man.

Then the chief had an idea. He took one of the sick children from her mother. With the child in his arms, he walked slowly toward the house. The farmer looked skeptical, but his wife, who had been watching from a window, came out.

"I think they're just hungry, Tom." Then she made signs with her hands to look like she was eating.

Standing Bear smiled and said to his followers, "We have done the right thing. These are good people. They will help us."

He took out his money, $20, and offered it to the farmer.

"Aw, keep your money, old man," the farmer said, but Standing Bear did not understand. So the farmer just ignored the offer. "Jane, get these people some food," he said, and his daughter came out of the house with a loaf of bread.

The Smiths watched their guests as they divided the bread into 31 equal pieces with a hunting knife and passed it around. Each of the Poncas hungrily ate half of his or her piece and put the other half into their bags. They had not eaten in two days. Standing Bear smiled in thanks, tried again to give the man some money, then turned around and started to walk away.

Tom Smith shouted to the group, "Hey, come back! There's more where that came from."

The Poncas did not understand what the man was saying, but they turned around to see why he was shouting. Standing Bear thought the farmer had changed his mind about the money, so he offered it again.

"Dog gone it, I don't want your money. Food! Do you understand 'food'?" But the Poncas did not understand. Mrs. Smith came to help her husband. She brought some eggs out of the house and pointed to a table under a tree. "Thanks, Sarah, I didn't know how to tell them they could stay."

The Smiths did not have a lot themselves, but they shared their food with Standing Bear and the others. As a way of saying thanks, the Indians sang some of their tribal songs for the family. Little Jane liked the hand game song best, and she learned the strange words very quickly. She played along with the children and moved her hands to go with the words.

While the others were singing and enjoying themselves, Standing Bear sneaked away and went to the wagon where his son's body was. He sat on the wagon next to the trunk and spoke to his son. "The people are happy again, son. We are going home. Soon you, too, will be home."

He then took his bag off the wagon and went with it to the others. He opened the bag and took out some papers. Mr.

Smith read one of the papers out loud. " 'The bearer of this paper is Ma-chu-na-zha (Standing Bear), one of the main chiefs of the Ponca tribe of Indians. He is a friend to the whites and is loyal to the government of the United States of America. He deserves respect and kind treatment. Signed: William H. Hugo, First Lieutenant, U.S. Army'."

Tom Smith pronounced the strange name on the paper again. "Ma-chu-na-zha. Is that your name?"

Standing Bear smiled and pointed to his heart. "Ma-chu-na-zha," he said. Then he pointed to the man's heart and looked at him with a question in his eyes.

"Tom Smith. I'm Tom Smith."

"Tom Smith," the chief repeated and smiled. "Tom Smith." The two men put their arms around each other and said each other's names, the only words each knew in the other's language.

The Poncas spent the night in the Smiths' barn, and the next day each of them got a small loaf of bread from Sarah Smith, who had stayed up all night and baked. Little Jane gave each of the children an egg or a toy.

The Smiths and the Poncas did not need words for their goodbyes. Everybody smiled and hugged and waved. Standing Bear knew he should not offer them money again, as these were good people. "Tom Smith," Standing Bear said.

"Ma-chu-na-zha," answered Tom Smith.

"Do you think they'll make it, Tom?" asked Sarah as the group disappeared in the distance.

"I don't know, Sarah. Heck, we don't even know where they're going."

Over the next few weeks, Standing Bear and his group met all kinds of white people. Some helped the Poncas, others ran after them with guns. But the ones who helped were very nice, and most would not take the Indians' money.

One morning, just as they were leaving a farmhouse, a group of soldiers rode toward the house. The old couple who lived on the farm saw the fear in the Poncas' eyes when they saw the soldiers in the distance. They reacted quickly.

"Mary Lou, take them into the barn," said the farmer.

When the soldiers came, the man greeted them. "What can I do for the army today, boys?"

"You can let our horses have some water, old man," answered the young officer.

While the horses were drinking, the officer suddenly asked, "By the way, you didn't see any Indians around here in the last few days, did you?"

"Indians? No, there haven't been Indians around here for years."

"Yeah, well, some Indians escaped from Indian Territory a few weeks ago, and Washington thinks they might be coming this way. If you see 'em, you be careful. They're dangerous."

"Oh, I'll be careful, young man. Don't worry about me." Dangerous? he thought. Not that poor group in his barn. When the soldiers were gone, Mary Lou and Jack Weston insisted that the Poncas stay another night.

And so it went for ten long weeks. Then, in mid-March, 1879, Standing Bear and his party arrived at the reservation of their friends, the Omaha, in Nebraska. They were very tired and hungry, and by now only two people were not sick. But all 31 had survived the journey. Only a horse had died. The other one had to be shot as soon as the group arrived in Nebraska. But it had done its job. The bones of Standing Bear's son were almost home.

CHAPTER FIVE

When the party of Poncas arrived at the Omaha reservation, the Omahas were plowing their fields to get them ready for the spring wheat. Yellow Smoke was the first to see Standing Bear and his group. He let his plow fall and ran to them.

"Standing Bear! Welcome. I thought you were in Indian Territory."

"Yellow Smoke, my friend. We *were* in Indian Territory. We have been walking for ten weeks. Soon we will be home."

"Your home is with us for now. You and your people will stay with the Omaha until you are strong again. Wait here, I will fetch some wagons."

Yellow Smoke ran to the village in the center of the reservation and told the others that Standing Bear had returned. Nine men drove their wagons to meet the Poncas and to take them to the village. The Poncas and the Omahas had been friends for many years, and their tribes spoke the same language. Many Poncas and Omahas had married over the years. The people were excited. Maybe some of their relatives were among the group.

When Standing Bear and his people were finally in the village and had warmed up, the Omahas had a big welcome feast in their honor. But most of the Poncas were too sick to eat. Still, they were happy to be among friends and so close to home.

Bright Eyes, a young Omaha woman who knew the language of the white men, said, "We will celebrate another time, Standing Bear, when your people are well. I will ride to the agency office and arrange for a doctor to come."

After Bright Eyes had gone, the Poncas told their story. They told the Omaha about their long march to Indian Territory, how the soldiers had watched them. They told of the many deaths on the way to Indian Territory. And they told their friends about the conditions there. That they had not been given any work to do. That they got there too late in the year to plant crops for food. That so many had died.

They talked about the sickness that had made them too weak to bury their dead. And they said that they had used their horses to pull the dead out onto the prairie to rot. Many of the Omaha cried openly when they heard about the suffering of the Poncas, and when they heard that friends or relatives had died. But the Poncas themselves did not cry. They had learned that crying could not bring back the dead. And many of them thought that the dead were perhaps better off than they were. The living still had to suffer; for the dead, the suffering was over.

Bright Eyes came back from the agency office about an hour later. "The doctor will be here in a few minutes. He will look after you, but he says that you must pay him for his services. You are not Omaha, and he is only paid to heal the Omaha."

Hard-Walker spoke first. "The Poncas are our guests here, and the doctor will treat them just as he would treat any of us."

"I'm afraid it's not that simple," Bright Eyes explained. "Although we live on this land, it belongs to the government. Only the government can give permission for the Poncas to stay here."

"Land cannot belong to anyone, Bright Eyes. That is a white man's way of looking at the world. We are here, just as we have always been here. And if we wish the Poncas to stay, they can stay."

Standing Bear stopped the argument. "We do not want you to get into trouble because of us. Please, we will pay for the doctor's services. Here, this is all the money we have."

Bright Eyes did not want to hurt the old man's pride. She took the money, a little over $1. "I will do that, Standing Bear. The doctor might try to cheat you." She knew that she would have to pay the doctor out of her own money, money that she

Standing Bear (about 1877)

had saved from cleaning the house of the white man who was in charge of the agency. But that did not matter. The Poncas were brothers.

While the doctor was with the sick Poncas, Bright Eyes talked to Yellow Smoke and Hard-Walker. The two men had been chiefs when the Omaha had still had chiefs, and the Omaha even now looked to them for help and advice.

"Mr. Vore says there is going to be trouble. He received a telegram from Washington weeks ago. He has been told to arrest the Poncas if they come here."

"But why, Bright Eyes?" asked Yellow Smoke. "I have told Standing Bear that he and his people are our guests here."

"Of course they are," said Hard-Walker. "They can stay as long as they want. We have more than enough land, and when they are strong, they can each use some to grow food and support themselves. Next season, they can go back to the land of their fathers."

"If only it was that easy, Hard-Walker. I want the Poncas to stay, too. But they will be arrested if they do," explained Bright Eyes. "I've asked Mr. Vore to wait as long as he can before he arrests them or tells the soldiers they are here."

"You have done well, Bright Eyes," said Yellow Smoke.

"How much time do we have?" asked Hard-Walker.

"I don't know. Mr. Vore is a good man, but he has a job to do. I'm sure he will wait as long as he can."

"Tomorrow we will start to get the land ready for our friends," decided Hard-Walker. "They will help us as soon as they are strong enough."

"Yes, Hard-Walker. If the soldiers see that the Poncas are working hard to support themselves, they will not arrest them."

But Bright Eyes did not look like she believed her old chief's optimistic words.

Chapter Six

The next day, the Omaha told the Poncas that they could have land. They gave them tools and seed, and the reservation police helped Standing Bear and the others with the planting.

By the end of the first week, many acres of spring wheat had been planted for the Poncas. Most of the sick Poncas were feeling better by now, but they still had chills and fever. But they insisted on helping to work in the fields. The Poncas were happy again, and they nearly forgot that the soldiers were still looking for them.

On Sunday, March 23, the Poncas went to church to hear Reverend Dorsey speak. After the service, they went to the cabin which the Omaha had given Standing Bear. Sunday was a day of rest, but they wanted to have a meeting.

Just as everyone was sitting down, Bright Eyes ran into the room. "The soldiers are here, Standing Bear. They have come to arrest you."

"The soldiers are my friends, Bright Eyes," the old man replied. "Now let us begin our meeting."

But before the meeting could start, a young army lieutenant walked in. He was a tall, thin man with yellow hair and beard, no more than 25 years old. He did not look happy about what he had come to do.

"Standing Bear, I have come to ...," the lieutenant began.

"Lieutenant Carpenter, welcome to my new home," interrupted the old chief in his own language. Bright Eyes translated.

"The government doesn't agree with you, Standing Bear. You and your people are here without permission."

"Do I need permission to be with my friends, the Omaha? Am I a child?" asked Standing Bear.

"I have orders to arrest you and your group and bring you all to Fort Omaha," the lieutenant said. He did not want to answer the old Indian's question.

"Lieutenant Carpenter, my people have suffered enough. We want only to live in peace in the land of our fathers. I have come to bury my son here. He died, like so many others in what you call Indian Territory.

"I have always been a friend of the white people. You know I have been a good friend of the soldiers, too. Long before you came to Nebraska, I found a young soldier on my people's land. It was the middle of winter, and the poor boy was cold, frightened and starving. He should not have been on our land, but I carried him on my back for four miles to our camp. My people gave him food and drink. For weeks we tried to save the poor boy's life, but we could not.

"That is the kind of friend I am to the soldiers. And now you, a soldier, come here to drive me from the land of my fathers?"

"Standing Bear, I don't like this any more than you do, but I have my orders. Now, please. Come with me peacefully."

"Yes, Lieutenant," replied Standing Bear weakly. "We will go." He got up from the floor where he had been sitting the whole time and gave a signal for his people to follow.

When they were outside, the Poncas saw that Lieutenant Carpenter had not come alone. There were 20 armed soldiers with him. The army meant business. The kind lieutenant told the Indians that they could fetch their things from their cabins and tents. Quietly, one after the other, the Poncas went to get their things. Only Long Runner refused to go. He asked Bright Eyes to tell the soldiers to shoot him. It was better than going back to Indian Territory.

The soldiers did not shoot Long Runner. They tied him up and held a gun to his head. He would have to march with the others, but he would not be allowed to take his things with him.

Reverend Dorsey tried to protest against the arrest, but Lieutenant Carpenter only said, "I'm the wrong person to talk to, Reverend. I received my orders from General Crook."

Group portrait of Ponca chiefs and interpreters (Standing Bear is the third from the left in the front row)

"But why would the general order these arrests?" asked the Reverend. "He is a good man and has always been a friend of our red brothers."

"Even a general has to follow orders, Reverend," was the young soldier's reply. "I'd suggest you send your protest to Washington."

At noon the Poncas began their march to Fort Omaha. Lieutenant Carpenter decided to leave one sick old woman behind. He was afraid that she would die on the way to the fort.

Reverend Dorsey watched the group as they were taken away by the soldiers. In his protest to Washington he wrote that the Indians had left "without a struggle, save that which was going on in their own hearts".

When they arrived at Fort Omaha, the Poncas were very tired. Standing Bear asked at once to see General Crook, but the general was not at the fort. The old chief was going to lie down to rest, but he was interrupted by a knock on the door of the small room he and his wife lived in.

Standing Bear opened the door. On the other side waited a small, balding man with a funny moustache. The man spoke through an interpreter; he said he wanted to talk to Standing Bear. Because he was a polite man, Standing Bear let him in.

"Standing Bear, my name is Thomas Tibbles. I'm the assistant editor over at the *Omaha Daily Herald.* That's a newspaper here. I'd like to talk to you about your arrest."

"That would not be right," answered Standing Bear. "I have not been able to talk to General Crook yet. I should do that before I talk to anyone else."

"But I can help you, Standing Bear. When the American public hears what is happening here, there will be such a protest, the army won't be able to hold you."

"My differences are with the general, and I will settle them with him."

"But General Crook can't help you. I've asked a lot of questions, and they tell me the general was ordered to arrest you. There's nothing he can do to help you."

"Then I will talk to someone who can help me. It will cause trouble if I talk to someone else about my business with the army. I do not want to cause trouble." The chief got up from where he had been sitting and opened the door. "Now, Mr. Tibbles, if you will excuse us, my wife and I would like to rest."

Mr. Tibbles was almost out the door when he remembered something. He had once been very good friends with an Apache chief. The Apache had taught him a secret sign which showed him to be a special friend of the Indians. He did not know whether a Ponca would know the sign, but he tried it anyway.

Standing Bear's eyes lit up when he saw the sign. He put his arms around Mr. Tibbles and asked him to come back into the room. Then he sent his wife to get Buffalo Chip. The three men smoked a pipe of peace while Buffalo Chip told Mr. Tibbles everything.

Five hours later, Mr. Tibbles knew what he had to do. First he visited all the churches in the area. That same day, all the churches in Omaha wrote a telegram to Carl Schurz, who was Secretary of the Interior and responsible for Indian affairs. They wrote that the Poncas should be set free. They would never receive a reply to their telegram.

Chapter Seven

At noon on March 30, 1879, General Crook asked Standing Bear and his people to see him in his office. The editor was given permission to come, too. When everyone was already in the general's office, Standing Bear appeared. Mr. Tibbles was surprised to see that Standing Bear was wearing the full ceremonial costume of a Ponca chief: a red blanket with blue stripes, a beaded belt and a necklace of bear claws.

Standing Bear began to speak: "My people lived near here for many generations. When the white men came, we were their friends. You know that. Many years ago, the other chiefs and I signed a treaty with the Great Father in Washington."

"You mean the President?" asked the general.

"Yes, that is what you call him. The treaty said that we could live in the land of our fathers as long as we made no trouble. We did as we were told. Our children went to school, and many of us went to church and prayed to the white God. Then one day some men came. They said the Great Father had sent them, and that the Great Father wanted us to move south – to Indian Territory.

"We said we did not want to move, but we agreed to look at the land in Indian Territory. If we liked it, we would move. The men took ten chiefs there and showed us the land, but we did not like it. We have learned to farm, and the land there was no good for farming. But the men said we had to move, and when we refused, they left us there without money and without an interpreter. We had to walk back.

"When we got back, we sent a telegram to the Great Father. We asked him for help. But instead the soldiers came and forced us to go to Indian Territory. We had to leave our houses, which we had built with our own hands. We could not even take our farming tools with us. We lived in Indian Territory for months without getting food from the agency. We had to beg for food among the other Indians there. We even had to beg for work to do. The Poncas are a proud people, and we work hard. We do not like to have to beg.

"Finally I went to Washington and met with the Great Father. He was shocked when I told him what had happened to my people, but he said I should go back to Indian Territory. There I could choose the best land. I did, and my people started to farm. But sickness came, and 157 of my people died. Many were only children. I myself lost two children, one on the way to Indian Territory, one in Indian Territory. I have come to bury my son in the land of my fathers. I want to stay, just as the treaty with the Great Father says I can do. Please do not make me go back."

After his speech to the general, Standing Bear turned to the soldiers who were there in the room. "My friends and brothers," he began, "I want only to save myself and my tribe. If I saw a great fire on the prairie, I would take up my babies and run to save their lives. If I saw a river that was going to run over its banks, I would take my people and move to high ground. In Indian Territory I am faced with sickness and death. I want only to save my people from these dangers. Please, help me to save the lives of our women and children."

The general said, "I have heard all this before. Everything Standing Bear has said today is true. I have reported the whole story to Washington. I could report it again, but that might make things worse.

"Standing Bear, yours is a very hard case, and I would like to help you. But I have received an order from Washington, and I must do as I am told. I'm afraid there's nothing I can do for you. You and your people may stay here at the fort for two weeks, until you are strong enough to travel. We will give you enough food and water for the trip back to Indian Territory, and you may take your tools and your animals with you this time. Good luck, Standing Bear. May God be with you."

The soldiers all looked very sad as they brought the Poncas out of the room. Mr. Tibbles was already out the door, when the general called out to him. "Mr. Tibbles, have you got a few minutes?"

"Of course, General Crook," answered the editor and closed the door so no one else could hear what business the two had to discuss.

Thomas Tibbles knew he had a lot to do and only two weeks to do it. He went back to the offices of his newspaper and wrote the best article of his life about the troubles of the Ponca Indians. He spent a whole week's wages to telegraph his article to some of the more important newspapers in New York and Chicago. Then he sat down with some law books and began to read.

After a few hours of looking at law books, Mr. Tibbles thought he had found the answer. He would find a lawyer to take the case of the Poncas and ask a judge for a writ of habeas corpus. The government would then have to prove that it had good reasons for keeping the Indians prisoner. If it could not prove that it had good reasons, the Poncas would have to be set free. And he knew just the lawyer to talk to...

John Webster was a fairly young man, but he was known as an excellent lawyer. He had even been president of the constitutional convention of Nebraska, and he had gone to university with Thomas Tibbles.

"It won't work, Tom," was Webster's response when Tibbles explained his idea about the writ of habeas corpus. "Let me tell you about habeas corpus. It means that the government has to bring an arrested person into court. Then it has to prove that it has good reasons for keeping him in prison."

"Are you trying to tell me that you think the government had a good reason for arresting the Poncas, Jack?" protested Tibbles.

"No, that's not the point. I'm talking about *people* who are arrested, but, in the eyes of the law, an Indian is not a person."

"Jack, I've heard Standing Bear speak. He's a better person than most of the white men I know."

Webster tried to be patient with his friend. "I'm sure he is, from everything you've told me, Tom. But the Indians are wards of the state. They're not citizens. The state can do with them anything it wants. No court is going to say that Indians have rights like white people, whether we think that's right or not."

"So you're not even going to try?"

"I didn't say that, Tom. Let's go talk to Andrew Poppleton. If he thinks we can win this one, dog gone it, we'll try."

Chapter Eight

It took more than two hours for Tibbles, Webster and Poppleton to convince Standing Bear of their plan.

"But, Standing Bear," explained Webster, "you would not really be going against the general. General Crook is just the person we have to name in the petition to the court. We are really going against the U.S. Army."

That did not help to convince Standing Bear. "I have no argument with the army. I only want to live in the land of my fathers."

"Think of it as a sport, Standing Bear," tried Tibbles. "Indian boys, when they come of age, fight each other to see who is the strongest. But they do not try to hurt each other because they are brothers, friends."

"I would not fight General Crook. I know he is stronger."

Andrew Poppleton, who was much older than Tibbles and Webster, asked the two to leave the room. "I'd like to be alone with the chief," he said.

Mr. Poppleton sat down on the floor next to Standing Bear. He lit his pipe and said nothing for several minutes, then he offered his pipe to the chief. Standing Bear accepted the offer with a smile. In a voice so low that the interpreter could hardly hear him, Poppleton began to speak.

"Standing Bear, I respect you. I understand that you do not want to take General Crook to court. Our legal system is very strange in many ways. What we are asking you to do is not easy. All we want is this: we want to prove that you are a human being, and that you have rights.

"It is not a fight between two boys. It is not a sport. It is a question of principle. I know from talking with you for the last few hours that you have principles. In our courts, questions of principle are decided. Two men who both have principles, don't always agree about those principles. We let our courts decide when that happens. The court does not say, 'You are right and he is wrong.' It says, 'This principle is right, and that one is not.' Then the two men shake hands and do whatever the court decides.

"If you agree to take General Crook to court, he will not be angry with you. He has grown up in this system, and he knows that it is a better way to settle an argument than with his gun. He will respect you, and he will respect the decision of the court. And I know you will, too."

Standing Bear was silent for several minutes. Finally he answered with only four words: "I will do it."

The next day, Poppleton and Webster rode to Lincoln to see Judge Elmer Dundy and give him the petition with the 30 "X's", the signatures of the Poncas who had been arrested. The judge issued the writ of habeas corpus the same day. The government had three weeks to bring the Poncas to Lincoln, where it would have to prove that it had good reason for arresting them. Lawyers for both sides began three long, difficult weeks of preparation.

During the weeks before the trial, newspapers all over the country published their own opinions and letters from their readers in favor of the Poncas. The Omahas wrote a letter to the newspapers; they said they would be happy to give some of their land to their friends the Poncas. As one paper wrote: "These may have been savages at one time, but now they have overtaken us and moved into a position of honor."

Everything was going well for the Ponca case until E. A. Hayt, the Indian Commissioner in Washington, published an open letter to Secretary of the Interior Carl Schurz. In it he wrote, "By the treaty of 1868 the Sioux were given lands which included the Ponca reservation. As the Sioux and the Poncas are enemies, it was necessary to move the Poncas to Indian Territory to protect them.

"When I visited the tribe in Indian Territory, I found that they were very healthy. Only Standing Bear complained all the time and showed a bad spirit. Now he has left Indian Territory without permission and is trying to get public sympathy by lying about the condition of the tribe."

When Mr. Tibbles showed Standing Bear the letter, the old man was angry. "Mr. Hayt says our lands were given to the Sioux. Who had the right to give away our lands? The land was given to us by treaty, and neither the Commissioner nor anyone else could give it away. The Poncas were never asked if they would give away their land, and we never would have agreed to do that. How would the Commissioner feel if somebody gave his land to the Sioux?

"He says my people are healthy. How does he explain the many deaths in my tribe? Look at the small group of Poncas that are here. The army doctors will tell you how sick they are.

"Then he says I have a bad spirit. He must have changed his mind about me. I will show you a paper Mr. Hayt signed once, and you can decide whether he told the truth then or now."

Standing Bear went to his old trunk and took out a piece of paper with a big wax seal. The paper was signed by Commissioner Wayt two years before: "Standing Bear is a chief of the Ponca tribe. This tribe is living in peace with the United States. Standing Bear has helped to preserve peace and harmony between his people and the United States and has earned the confidence of all persons he may meet."

Mr. Tibbles said, "Mr. Hayt gave you a very good character in that letter."

"No," replied Standing Bear, who did not understand what Tibbles meant. "Mr. Hayt did not give me my good character. I have worked hard all my life for the good of my tribe. That has given me my good character. Mr. Hayt only wrote what he knew is true."

Chapter Nine

On May 1, 1879, the sun shone brightly on the little white courthouse in Lincoln. Over a hundred people were waiting outside the courthouse when the doors were opened at 8 o'clock. Besides a group of Omaha Indians who wanted to be there for their friends the Poncas, Reverend Dorsey and other members of the clergy had come. Reporters had traveled from as far away as Chicago to watch and report on the trial. Everybody seemed to be on the Poncas' side.

At 9 o'clock the trial began. Lieutenant Carpenter and his men led the prisoners into the courtroom. All of them were wearing white men's clothes – everyone except Standing Bear. The chief was wearing the complete dress of a Ponca chief, including a headdress and a necklace of bear claws. It was a wonderful sight, but Mr. Webster was not happy. He turned to Mr. Poppleton and said, "That's the end of the case. Didn't you explain to him that we must prove the Poncas are trying to live like white men?"

"I did. But maybe this isn't such a bad thing..."

If Judge Dundy was surprised, he did not show it. He entered the room and called the court to order. "Are all parties in the case of Standing Bear versus General George Crook, United States Army, present?"

"Yes, your honor," answered Mr. Webster and Mr. Poppleton, who were representing Standing Bear, and Mr. Lambertson, who was representing the government, at the same time. General Crook asked for permission to speak.

"Your honor, I do not think my name should be used in this trial. It was not my decision to arrest Standing Bear and his group. The people who gave me my orders should be on trial here."

The judge was very patient with the general. "General Crook, no one is on trial here. This is not a criminal case. We

Standing Bear in the complete dress of a Ponca chief

are here to decide whether you had the right to arrest the Poncas..."

"But, sir," the general interrupted.

"General, even if it was not your decision to make the arrests, you were in charge of the men who arrested Standing Bear and his party. Therefore, you must be named in this trial. I will be happy, however, to remember that you ordered the arrests only because you were ordered to do so."

"Thank you, your honor."

"Now, let's begin. Mr. Webster, Mr. Poppleton, you may call your first witness."

"Thank you, your honor," Mr. Webster replied. "Our first witness is Mr. Willie W. Hamilton."

Willie Hamilton owned the store at the Omaha Agency, and he spoke the language of the Omaha and the Poncas. Mr. Webster asked him a lot of questions about the condition of the Poncas and about how they had lived during their few weeks with the Omaha. Hamilton explained that the Poncas had been very sick when they had arrived, but that they were now much better. Most of them had helped to plant wheat and do other work on the reservation.

Mr. Lambertson asked questions about the structure of the tribe. "Standing Bear is their main chief, sir."

"So the people listen to Standing Bear?" asked Lambertson.

"Yes, they do."

"Then they do not live like white men?"

"Oh, they try to, sir."

"What day of the week was it when the Poncas were arrested?"

"Sunday."

"And were the Poncas working, or were they taking a day of rest, like Christians?"

"They were resting."

"And do they go to church, Mr. Hamilton?"

"I guess they're really a lot like white men, sir. Some go to church, some don't."

There was a lot of laughter in the courtroom, and Judge Dundy told everyone to be quiet. Reverend Dorsey was laughing so hard that he had to leave the room. It was not going to be easy for Mr. Lambertson to prove that the Poncas were not like white men.

The next witness was Lieutenant Carpenter. He reported that the Indians had been very sick, but that some had offered to work at the fort while they were there under arrest. He said that the Poncas had been cooperative and had caused no trouble. Then Mr. Webster called Standing Bear as his next witness.

Mr. Lambertson objected. "Your honor! Does the court think an Indian can be called as a witness?"

"The court does, Mr. Lambertson. If an Indian can be arrested, he can certainly be called as a witness."

Standing Bear spoke through an interpreter. He swore on the Bible that he would tell "the truth, the whole truth, and nothing but the truth, so help me God."

Standing Bear told the court the story of his tribe. He told them how the Poncas' land had been taken away without their permission. He told them how many of his people had died down in Indian Territory, and that he had brought his son's body back north to be buried in the land of their fathers.

"That is where I want to live for the rest of my life, too," Standing Bear said. "That is where I want to be buried. I want to go to my own land, where I will work until I am old and blind. But that will not change my color. I will always be an Indian in color. But maybe I can become a citizen."

"Then you want to live like white men?" Mr. Webster asked.

"Like which white men, Mr. Webster?"

"Well, like civilized men..."

"Mr. Webster, I have traveled a lot over the years. I have met many white men. Some work very hard, build houses, farm land that was once wilderness. I would like to be like those white men. But there are other white men who are lazy. They drink and make trouble. I do not want to be like those white men."

"But you are the chief and head man of your people, are you not?" Mr. Lambertson asked.

"No, not any more," Standing Bear answered. "I do not consider myself any better than the rest. I am as poor as the rest of my people."

"Your people still come to you for help and advice, do they not?" continued Lambertson.

"Yes, they do. I was their chief for many years, and my people trust me. But now they do not come to me as their chief. They know I am their friend. If they think I can help, they come to me. But why do you ask all these questions? I only want my land back. Land that was taken from my people without permission..."

But Judge Dundy did not let Standing Bear go on. "You are not here to ask questions, Standing Bear, but only to answer them. Now, it's getting late. We will meet again at 9 o'clock tomorrow morning."

The first day of the trial was over. Webster and Tibbles were worried, but Poppleton seemed happy with the way the day had gone. "We have the training, but Standing Bear is our best hope. You two should get some rest. Tomorrow is going to be a long day."

Chapter Ten

The next morning the trial began again at 9 o'clock sharp. Mr. Webster said that he had no more witnesses, so the judge asked Mr. Lambertson to call his.

"The government does not want to call any witnesses, your honor," Lambertson said.

Even Judge Dundy could not hide his surprise. "Are you sure, Mr. Lambertson?"

"Yes, your honor. We are here to decide a question of law, and the government believes that witnesses are not necessary."

"Well then," the judge said, "let's hear your closing arguments. Are you ready, Mr. Webster?"

"We are, your honor."

Mr. Webster spoke for a long time. He talked about how badly the white men had treated the Indians. Then he gave a summary of the terrible things that had been done to the Poncas. At the end of his arguments he explained that the government had had no right to take away the Poncas' land.

"There are only three ways to get land under the law: one can discover it, one can conquer it, and one can buy it. Let us consider these three possibilities. First of all, discovery. When the white men landed on this continent, that did not give them land where other people were already living. The land had already been 'discovered' by the Indians. We could only take land that nobody lived on, and we could take political control. But that does not mean that the land belonged to us.

"The second possibility is by conquest. The United States government did not conquer the Poncas. There was never even a war between the United States and the Poncas. In fact, the two peoples have lived in peace and even been friends. Standing Bear's relationship with the army has always been a good one."

General Crook nodded his head as Mr. Webster continued. "And as far as the third possibility is concerned, the United

States has never even tried to give the Poncas money for the land the government took from them. And the Poncas have made it quite clear that they would not accept money for their land. In order to buy something from somebody, that person must agree to sell.

"We can see that none of the three possibilities for getting land legally is the case here. It is obvious, then, that the government took the Poncas' land illegally."

Mr. Poppleton talked for some time about habeas corpus. He said that habeas corpus included Indians because Indians were human beings. There could be no doubt that Standing Bear, who had spoken here at the trial, was a man. And as a man, he had rights. At the end of his speech he said, "If the law decides that Standing Bear is not a man in the sense of the law, then there is something wrong with the law. Then I do not want to be a man under this law either."

After lunch it was Mr. Lambertson's turn to speak. "Your honor, before I make my closing argument, I would like to compliment Mr. Poppleton and Mr. Webster for taking on this case. They are receiving no money, and I feel it is very noble of them to want to help these helpless Indians. But, of course, they cannot help the Poncas, who are not people under the law, just as a Negro is not a person under the law. The highest court in our great nation said so in the 1857 Dred Scott case."

Lambertson went on to talk about different fine points of law. He spoke for nearly six hours. Then Standing Bear was allowed to speak. His short speech was interrupted several times by applause, although Judge Dundy had ordered the people to be quiet. "Although my skin is a different color," Standing Bear said, "I am a man. God made me, just as he made the white man. I am not a savage, but a friend. I want to be treated like a friend."

On May 12, 1879, Judge Dundy announced his decision in the case of Standing Bear versus General George Crook, United

States Army: "Ladies and Gentlemen, I have read a lot of law books over the past few weeks. But I have found another book more useful: *Webster's Dictionary.* One of the definitions of 'person' there is 'a living soul; a moral being'. We have heard Standing Bear speak during this trial, and there can be no doubt in our minds that he is a 'living soul'. His feelings for his people show that, just as his compassion shows that he is a 'moral being'.

"Therefore I find that an Indian is a person within the meaning of the law of the United States. In times of peace, no one, neither the government nor the army, has the right to transport Indians from one part of the country to another without their permission. No one has the right to force them to stay on a reservation if they do not want to be there. The Poncas will be released."

Just as Mr. Poppleton had promised, General Crook went to Standing Bear and shook his hand. Before he left the courtroom, the general saluted the old man in military style and gave a secret sign – the same sign Mr. Tibbles had used to show he was a friend of the Indians.

EPILOGUE

After their trial, Standing Bear and his group of Poncas went to live on some islands in the Niobrara River which had not been given to the Sioux. The conditions of the Poncas in Indian Territory had improved, and most of the Poncas who lived there decided to stay. About 170 came to live with Standing Bear in Nebraska.

Standing Bear lived in the land of his fathers until his death in 1908. Today there are still two separate groups of Poncas, about 400 in Nebraska and about 900 in Oklahoma.

Indians became citizens of the United States of America in 1924.

Vocabulary

AE = American English, *BE* = British English,
pl. = plural, *sb.* = somebody, *sth.* = something

A **acre** ['eɪkə] *Flächenmaß (= ca. 0,4 Hektar)*
affair [ə'feə] Angelegenheit
agency ['eɪdʒənsɪ] Amt
ahead of [ə'hed] vor
along [ə'lɒŋ] hier: zusammen
(to) **announce** [ə'naʊns] verkünden; ankündigen
applause [ə'plɔːz] Applaus, Beifall
argument ['ɑːgjʊmənt] Streit
argument: closing argument ['kləʊzɪŋ] Schlußplädoyer
armed [ɑːmd] bewaffnet
arrest [ə'rest] Verhaftung
arrest: under arrest verhaftet
(to) **arrest** [ə'rest] verhaften, festnehmen
as far as ... is concerned [kən'sɜːnd] was ... betrifft
(to) **assemble** [ə'sembl] sich versammeln

B (to) **bake** [beɪk] backen
balding [bɔːldɪŋ] mit schütterem Haar
bank [bæŋk] Ufer
barn [bɑːn] Scheune
beaded ['biːdɪd] perlenbesetzt
bearer ['beərə] Inhaber/in
(to) **beat down on** [biːt] daniederpeitschen auf
(to) **beg** [beg] betteln
being ['biːɪŋ] Wesen
being: human being [hjuːmən 'biːɪŋ] Mensch
belt [belt] Gürtel
besides [bɪ'saɪdz] außer
Bible ['baɪbl] Bibel

blind [blaɪnd] blind
bone [bəʊn] Knochen
bones [bəʊnz] Knochen; Gebeine
(to) **breathe on sth.** [bri:ð] etwas anhauchen
bucket ['bʌkɪt] Eimer
buffalo, *pl.:* **buffalo, buffalo(e)s** ['bʌfələʊ/z] Büffel

C **cabin** ['kæbɪn] Hütte
case [keɪs] Fall
ceremonial costume [serɪ'məʊnɪəl 'kɒstju:m] (Feder-) Schmuck und Kleidung für zeremonielle Anlässe
chapter ['tʃæptə] Kapitel
charge: (to) **be in charge of** [tʃɑ:dʒ] verantwortlich sein für
(to) **cheat sb.** [tʃi:t] jdn. betrügen
chief [tʃi:f] Häuptling
chills *(pl.)* [tʃɪlz] Schüttelfrost
Christian ['krɪstʃən] Christ/in
civilized ['sɪvəlaɪzd] zivilisiert
claw [klɔ:] Klaue
clergy ['klɜ:dʒɪ] Klerus, Geistlichkeit
closing argument [kləʊzɪŋ 'ɑ:gjʊmənt] Schlußplädoyer
commissioner [kə'mɪʃənə] Beauftragte/r
compassion [kəm'pæʃn] Mitgefühl
concerned: as far as ... is concerned [kən'sɜ:nd] was ... betrifft
condition [kən'dɪʃn] Zustand
confidence ['kɒnfɪdəns] Vertrauen
(to) **conquer** ['kɒŋkə] erobern
conquest ['kɒŋkwest] Eroberung
(to) **consider** [kən'sɪdə] betrachten
constitutional convention [kɒnstɪ'tju:ʃənl kən'venʃn] verfassunggebende Versammlung
cooperative [kəʊ'ɒpərətɪv] kooperativ

costume: ceremonial costume [serɪ'məʊnɪəl 'kɒstju:m] (Feder-)Schmuck und Kleidung für zeremonielle Anlässe
couple ['kʌpl] (Ehe-)Paar
court [kɔ:t] Gericht
courthouse ['kɔ:thaʊs] Gerichtsgebäude
courtroom ['kɔ:trʊm] Gerichtssaal
cover: under the cover of darkness ['kʌvə] im Schutz der Dunkelheit
crops [krɒps] Feldfrüchte
crunching sound ['krʌntʃɪŋ] knirschendes Geräusch

D **darkness** ['dɑ:knɪs] Dunkelheit
dead: the dead [ded] die Toten
dead: their dead die Toten unter ihnen
definition [defɪ'nɪʃn] Definition
(to) **deserve** [dɪ'zɜ:v] verdienen
detail ['di:teɪl] Detail
dim [dɪm] *(Licht)* schwach
(to) **disappear** [dɪsə'pɪə] verschwinden
(to) **discover** [dɪs'kʌvə] entdecken
discovery [dɪ'skʌvərɪ] Entdeckung
Dog gone it! [dɒg 'gɒn ɪt] Verflixt noch mal!
doorway ['dɔ:weɪ] Tür(öffnung)
doubt [daʊt] Zweifel
dress: the complete dress of a Ponca chief [dres] *hier:* vollständige Kleidung und Schmuck eines Ponca-Häuptlings
dried [draɪd] getrocknet

E **editor** ['edɪtə] Redakteur/in
epilogue ['epɪlɒg] Nachwort
evil ['i:vl] böse
excitement [ɪk'saɪtmənt] Aufregung

F **faced:** (to) **be faced with sth.** [feɪst] konfrontiert sein mit etwas
favor *(AE)* = **favour** *(BE):* (to) **be in favor of sb./sth.** ['feɪvə] für jdn./etwas sein
fear [fɪə] Angst, Furcht
feast [fi:st] Festessen
fever ['fi:və] Fieber
fine: fine point of law [faɪn] schwierige Rechtsfrage
follower ['fɒləʊə] Anhänger/in
(to) **forgive, forgave, forgiven** [fə'gɪv] vergeben; verzeihen
(to) **form** [fɔ:m] formen
fort [fɔ:t] Fort
fried [fraɪd] gebraten; fritiert

G **general** ['dʒenrəl] General
generation [dʒenə'reɪʃn] Generation; Menschenalter
gentleman, *pl.:* **gentlemen** ['dʒentlmən] Herr
God: May God be with you. [gɒd] Gott schütze Sie!
(to) **greet** [gri:t] grüßen
(to) **grow up** [grəʊ] aufwachsen
guess: I guess *(AE)* [ges] ich nehme an, ich denke

H **habeas corpus** → **writ of habeas corpus**
harmony ['hɑ:mənɪ] Harmonie, Eintracht
headdress ['hedrəs] Kopfschmuck
health [helθ] Gesundheit
heaven ['hevn] Himmel
Heck! [hek] Verdammt!
honor *(AE)* = **honour** *(BE)* ['ɒnə] Ehre
honor: in sb.'s honor jdm. zu Ehren
honor: your honor Euer Ehren
(to) **hug** [hʌg] umarmen
human being [hju:mən 'bi:ɪŋ] Mensch

hunt [hʌnt] Jagd
hunting knife [hʌntɪŋ ˌnaɪf] Jagdmesser

I **illegal** [ɪ'li:gl] illegal
imprisoned [ɪm'prɪznd] inhaftiert, gefangen
(to) **include** [ɪn'klu:d] einschließen, enthalten
including [ɪn'klu:dɪŋ] einschließlich, inklusive
Indian Territory ['terətrɪ] Indianer-Territorium *(Gebiet, etwa dem heutigen Bundesstaat Oklahoma gleich, das im 19. Jahrhundert von der US-Regierung den Indianern zugedacht wurde)*
(to) **insist: he insisted that they stay** [ɪn'sɪst] er bestand darauf, daß sie blieben
Interior: Secretary of the Interior ['sekrətrɪ, ɪn'tɪərɪə] *(USA)* Innenminister/in
(to) **interrupt** [ɪntə'rʌpt] unterbrechen
invention: of sb.'s invention [ɪn'venʃn] jds. Fantasie entsprungen
(to) **issue** ['ɪʃu:] erteilen

J **judge** [dʒʌdʒ] Richter/in

K **keep:** (to) **keep sb. prisoner** ['prɪznə] jdn. gefangenhalten

L **laid:** (to) **lay, laid, laid** [leɪ] (hin-)legen
Latin ['lætɪn] Latein
laughter ['lɑ:ftə] Gelächter
law: fine point of law [lɔ:] schwierige Rechtsfrage
lawyer: he knew just the lawyer to talk to ['lɔ:jə] er kannte genau den Anwalt, mit dem man reden mußte
legal ['li:gl] legal
legal system ['li:gl] Rechtssystem
(to) **lie** [laɪ] lügen

lieutenant [*AE:* luː'tenənt; *BE:* lef'tenənt] Leutnant
(to) **light, lit, lit** [laɪt, lɪt] anzünden
light: sb.'s eyes light up jds. Augen leuchten
living: the living die Lebenden
living soul [lɪvɪŋ 'səʊl] lebende Seele
loaf, *pl.:* **loaves** [ləʊf, ləʊvz] Laib (Brot)
lodge [lɒdʒ] Stammesgruppe
luck: Good luck. [lʌk] Viel Erfolg!
lying: by lying about the condition of his tribe ['laɪɪŋ, kən'dɪʃn] indem er über den Zustand seines Stammes Lügen verbreitet

M (to) **make it** es schaffen
(to) **make sb. do sth.** jdn. veranlassen/dazu bringen, etwas zu tun
march [mɑːtʃ] Marsch
(to) **march** [mɑːtʃ] marschieren
(to) **mean business** ['bɪznɪs] es ernst meinen
meaning: within the meaning of the law ['miːnɪŋ] im Sinne des Gesetzes
mild [maɪld] mild
military ['mɪlɪtrɪ] militärisch
mind: (to) **change one's mind** [maɪnd] seine Meinung ändern
mind: sth. rests heavily on sb.'s mind ['hevɪlɪ, maɪnd] etwas belastet einen sehr
moral being [mɒrəl 'biːɪŋ] moralisch denkendes Wesen
moustache [mə'stɑːʃ] Schnurrbart

N (to) **name** [neɪm] (be-)nennen
necklace ['neklɪs] Halskette
needy ['niːdɪ] bedürftig
Negro ['niːgrəʊ] Neger/in *(nur noch im historischen Kontext)*
neither … nor ['naɪðə, nɔː] weder … noch

no good: the land was no good for farming das Land war nicht für Ackerbau geeignet
noble ['nəʊbl] nobel, edel
none [nʌn] keine(r, s)
noon [nu:n] Mittag
nothing but ['nʌθɪŋ] nichts als

O (to) **object** [əb'dʒekt] Einspruch erheben
optimistic [ɒptɪ'mɪstɪk] optimistisch
order ['ɔ:də] Befehl
(to) **order** ['ɔ:də] befehlen, anordnen

P (to) **pack** [pæk] packen
party ['pɑ:tɪ] Gruppe; Partei
people ['pi:pl] *hier:* Volk
physical ['fɪzɪkl] körperlich
(to) **plant** [plɑ:nt] anbauen, anpflanzen
plow *(AE)* = **plough** *(BE)* [plaʊ] Pflug
(to) **plow** *(AE)* = (to) **plough** *(BE)* [plaʊ] pflügen
poor [pɔ:] ärmlich
prairie ['preərɪ] Prärie, Grasebene *(in Nordamerika)*
(to) **pray** [preɪ] beten
preparation [prepə'reɪʃn] Vorbereitung
present ['preznt] anwesend
(to) **preserve** [prɪ'zɜ:v] wahren
pride [praɪd] Stolz
principle ['prɪnsəpl] Prinzip
prisoner ['prɪznə] Gefangene/r
(to) **keep sb. prisoner** jdn. gefangenhalten
protest ['prəʊtest] Protest(schreiben)
(to) **prove** [pru:v] beweisen
public ['pʌblɪk] Öffentlichkeit
(to) **publish** ['pʌblɪʃ] veröffentlichen

puff [pʌf] Zug *(Zigarette, Pfeife)*
(to) **puff** [pʌf] ziehen *(Zigarette, Pfeife)*

R (to) **receive** [rɪ'siːv] bekommen
relationship [rɪ'leɪʃnʃɪp] Verhältnis
reply [rɪ'plaɪ] Antwort, Erwiderung
(to) **reply** [rɪ'plaɪ] antworten, erwidern
(to) **represent** [reprɪ'zent] vertreten
(to) **respect** [rɪ'spekt] respektieren
response [rɪ'spɒns] Antwort, Erwiderung
responsible for [rɪ'spɒnsəbl] verantwortlich für
rest [rest] Ruhe, Erholung
(to) **rest: sth. rests heavily on sb.'s mind** [rest, maɪnd] etwas belastet einen sehr
Reverend ['revərənd] *(Anrede)* Pfarrer
(to) **rot** [rɒt] verrotten

S (to) **salute** [sə'luːt] (militärisch) grüßen
savage ['sævɪdʒ] Wilde/r
save [seɪv] außer; bis auf
seal [siːl] Siegel
secret ['siːkrɪt] geheim, Geheim-
Secretary of the Interior ['sekrətrɪ, ɪn'tɪərɪə] *(USA)* Innenminister/in
seed [siːd] Samen
sense [sens] Sinn
service ['sɜːvɪs] Gottesdienst
services ['sɜːvɪsɪz] Dienste
(to) **set sb. free** jdn. freilassen
(to) **settle** ['setl] *hier:* beilegen
sharp: at 9 o'clock sharp [ʃɑːp] Punkt 9 Uhr
shocked [ʃɒkt] schockiert
shotgun ['ʃɒtgʌn] Schrotflinte
sick: the sick die Kranken
signature ['sɪgnətʃə] Unterschrift

signed [saɪnd] gezeichnet
silence ['saɪləns] Stille, Ruhe
silent ['saɪlənt] still, ruhig
since [sɪns] seit(dem)
skeptical *(AE)* = **sceptical** *(BE)* ['skeptɪkl] skeptisch
(to) **sneak away** [sniːk] sich davonstehlen
soul: living soul [səʊl] lebende Seele
speech [spiːtʃ] Rede
spirit ['spɪrɪt] Geist
spirit: he showed a bad spirit ['spɪrɪt] *hier:* er wollte sich mit seiner Lage nicht abfinden
spot [spɒt] Fleck; Ort
starving ['stɑːvɪŋ] ausgehungert, halb verhungert
structure ['strʌktʃə] Struktur, Aufbau
struggle ['strʌgl] Kampf
(to) **support oneself** [sə'pɔːt] seinen Unterhalt selbst bestreiten
surprise [sə'praɪz] Überraschung
swore: (to) **swear, swore, sworn** [sweə, swɔː, swɔːn] schwören
sympathy ['sɪmpəθɪ] Mitleid; Sympathie

T **telegram** ['telɪgræm] Telegramm
(to) **telegraph** ['telɪgrɑːf] telegrafieren
territory: Indian Territory ['terətrɪ] Indianer-Territorium *(Gebiet, etwa dem heutigen Bundesstaat Oklahoma gleich, das im 19. Jahrhundert von der US-Regierung den Indianern zugedacht wurde)*
therefore ['ðeəfɔː] deshalb
toward [tə'wɔːd] = **towards** [tə'wɔːdz] auf … zu; in Richtung auf
(to) **transport** [træns'pɔːt] transportieren
(to) **treat** [triːt] behandeln
treatment ['triːtmənt] Behandlung
treaty ['triːtɪ] Vertrag

trial ['traɪəl] Prozeß
trial: (to) **be on trial** unter Anklage stehen
trunk [trʌŋk] Truhe
(to) **trust** [trʌst] (ver-)trauen

V **versus** ['vɜːsəs] gegen

W **wagon = waggon** ['wægən] Pferdewagen
(to) **want sb. to do sth.** [wɒnt] wollen, daß jd. etwas tut
ward [wɔːd] Mündel
(to) **warm sth.** [wɔːm] etwas aufwärmen
(to) **warm up** sich aufwärmen
warrior ['wɒrɪə] Krieger/in
(to) **wave** [weɪv] winken
whatever [wɒt'evə] was auch immer
(to) **whistle** ['wɪsl] pfeifen
wilderness ['wɪldənɪs] Wildnis
wise [waɪz] weise
within the meaning of the law [wɪ'ðɪn] im Sinne des Gesetzes
without doing sth. ohne etwas zu tun
witness ['wɪtnɪs] Zeuge, Zeugin
writ of habeas corpus [rɪt, heɪbɪəs 'kɔːpəs] *richterlicher Befehl, nach dem ein/e Inhaftierte/r vor Gericht vorgeführt werden muß zwecks Erteilung eines Haftbefehls; anderenfalls ist die/der Inhaftierte freizulassen*

List of names

Carpenter	['kɑːpəntə]
Crook	[krʊk]
Du-ba-mo-ni	[duːbə'məʊnɪ]
Dorsey	['dɔːsɪ]
Dundy	['dʌndɪ]
Hamilton	['hæmltən]
Hayt	[heɪt]
Hugo	['hjuːgəʊ]
Lambertson	['læmbətsən]
Ma-chu-na-zha	[mɑːtʃuː'nɑːʒə]
Mary Lou	['meərɪ 'luː]
Poppleton	['pɒpltən]
Schurz	[ʃɜːts]
Suzette	[sʊ'zet]
Thomas	['tɒməs]
Tibbles	['tɪblz]
Vore	[vɔː]
Wakanda	[wə'kɑːndə]
Wakanda-pezi	[wə'kɑːndə 'pezɪ]
Webster	['webstə]
Weston	['westn]

Keya Paha	['kiːə 'pɑːhɑː]
Lincoln	['lɪŋkən]
Niobrara	[naɪə'breərə]

Apache/s	[ə'pætʃɪ/z]
Herald	['herəld]
Omaha/s	['əʊməhɑː/z]
Ponca/s	['pɒŋkə/z]
Sioux	[*sing.:* suː, *pl.:* suːz]
xúbe	['ʃuːbɪ]